ENDANGERED BEARS

Bobbie Kalman & Kylie Burns

Crabtree Publishing Company

www.crabtreebooks.com

Earth's Endangered Animals Series

A Bobbie Kalman Book

Dedicated by Kylie Burns

For my mom and dad, Jo-Ann and Lonnie Wright. I love you more than words could say.
Thank you for inspiring and encouraging me in everything I do. You make life sweet!

Editor-in-Chief
Bobbie Kalman

Writing team
Bobbie Kalman
Kylie Burns

Substantive editor
Kelley MacAulay

Editors
Molly Aloian
Michael Hodge
Rebecca Sjonger
Kathryn Smithyman

Photo research
Crystal Foxton

Design
Katherine Kantor
Margaret Amy Salter (cover)

Production coordinator
Heather Fitzpatrick

Consultant
Patricia Loesche, Ph.D., Animal Behavior Program,
Department of Psychology, University of Washington

Illustrations
Barbara Bedell: page 9 (sloth bear)
Bonna Rouse: back cover, pages 9 (giant panda, polar bear), 10, 15, 18
Margaret Amy Salter: pages 8, 9 (spectacled bear, sun bear, Asiatic black bear,
    and American black bear), 19, 23

Photographs
© Richard Sobol/Animals Animals - Earth Scenes: page 11
Bruce Coleman Inc.: M. Renner: page 29
Eric Horan/Index Stock: page 20
iStockphoto.com: Stefan Ekernas: page 1; Vladimir Pomortsev: page 18
Minden Pictures: ZSSD: page 30
Naturepl.com: Jim Clare: page 14; Philip Dalton: front cover; Laurent Geslin: page 21;
    Pete Oxford: page 24
Photo Researchers, Inc.: Terry Whittaker: page 25
© Steven Kazlowski/SeaPics.com: page 12
© ShutterStock.com/Mike Flippo: page 4
Visuals Unlimited: Inga Spence: page 23
Other images by Corel, Creatas, Digital Stock, Digital Vision, Eyewire, and Photodisc

Library and Archives Canada Cataloguing in Publication

Kalman, Bobbie, 1947-
    Endangered bears / Bobbie Kalman & Kylie Burns.

(Earth's endangered animals)
Includes index.
ISBN 978-0-7787-1861-1 (bound)
ISBN 978-0-7787-1907-6 (pbk.)

    1. Bears--Juvenile literature. 2. Endangered species--Juvenile
literature. I. Burns, Kylie II. Title. III. Series.

QL737.C27K3475 2007   j599.78   C2007-900531-4

Library of Congress Cataloging-in-Publication Data

Kalman, Bobbie.
    Endangered bears / Bobbie Kalman & Kylie Burns.
        p. cm. -- (Earth's endangered animals)
    Includes index.
    ISBN-13: 978-0-7787-1861-1 (rlb)
    ISBN-10: 0-7787-1861-1 (rlb)
    ISBN-13: 978-0-7787-1907-6 (pb)
    ISBN-10: 0-7787-1907-3 (pb)
    1. Bears--Juvenile literature. 2. Endangered species--Juvenile literature.
I. Burns, Kylie. II. Title. III. Series.
    QL737.C27K352 2007
    599.78--dc22

                                        2007002688

Crabtree Publishing Company

www.crabtreebooks.com   1-800-387-7650

Published in Canada
Crabtree Publishing
616 Welland Ave.
St. Catharines, ON
L2M 5V6

Published in the United States
Crabtree Publishing
PMB16A
350 Fifth Ave., Suite 3308
New York, NY 10118

Published in the United Kingdom
Crabtree Publishing
White Cross Mills
High Town, Lancaster
LA1 4XS

Published in Australia
Crabtree Publishing
386 Mt. Alexander Rd.
Ascot Vale (Melbourne)
VIC 3032

Contents

Endangered bears

Many animals on Earth are **endangered**. Endangered animals are at risk of disappearing from Earth forever. Most **species**, or types, of bears are endangered or **vulnerable**.

Bears need help

People must protect bears so that they do not become **extinct**. Extinct animals no longer live anywhere on Earth. Keep reading to find out why so many bears are endangered and how people can help them.

Giant pandas are endangered bears.

Words to know

Scientists use certain words to describe animals that are in danger. Some of these words are listed below.

vulnerable Describes animals that may soon become endangered

endangered Describes animals that are in danger of dying out in the **wild**

critically endangered Describes animals that are at high risk of dying out in the wild

extinct Describes animals that are no longer known to live anywhere on Earth

What are bears?

Bears are **mammals**. Mammals are **warm-blooded** animals. All mammals have backbones. Most mammals also have hair or fur on their bodies. Baby mammals **nurse**, or drink milk from the bodies of their mothers.

Bear facts

Bears belong to a group of mammals called the **Ursidae family**. Bears are the only animals in this family. Bears have large, strong bodies. They also have short legs, small round ears, and short tails.

Marine mammals

Polar bears are the only bears that are **marine mammals**. Marine mammals are mammals that live mainly in oceans. Polar bears spend most of their time on ice that floats in oceans. Polar bears find food in oceans, too. In summer, the bears also look for food on land. As a result, some scientists believe that polar bears are both marine mammals and land mammals.

Eight kinds of bears

There are eight species of bears. Asiatic black bears, giant pandas, sloth bears, and sun bears live in different parts of Asia. Spectacled bears live in South America. American black bears live throughout most of North America. Brown bears live mainly in the northern parts of North America and Asia, as well as in small parts of Europe. Polar bears live in the **Arctic**. The Arctic includes the Arctic Ocean and the northern **coasts** of North America, Europe, and Asia.

Many kinds

There are several kinds of certain bear species. Two kinds of brown bears live in North America—grizzly bears and Kodiak bears. There are also several kinds of North American black bears and Asiatic black bears. Using an atlas, find the homes of the bears on these two pages.

Most brown bears live in Alaska, Canada, and Russia. This brown bear is a Kodiak bear.

8

Sun bears live mainly in China and **Indochina** *(see glossary, page 32).*

Spectacled bears live mainly in Venezuela, Colombia, and Peru.

Asiatic black bears live in many Asian countries, including India, China, Thailand, and Pakistan.

Polar bears live in the most northern parts of Alaska, Canada, Greenland, and Russia.

Giant pandas live only in China.

American black bears live in Canada, the United States, and Mexico.

Sloth bears live in Asian countries such as India, Nepal, and Sri Lanka.

Bear habitats

A **habitat** is the natural place where an animal lives. Bears live in many habitats, such as forests, **rain forests**, **grasslands**, and **tundra**. Many bears, including spectacled bears, giant pandas, Asiatic black bears, and some brown bears, live in forests that grow on mountains.

Hot and cold

Different bear species live in habitats with different **climates**. For example, sun bears live in hot rain forests, whereas polar bears live mainly on ice that floats in the freezing Arctic Ocean.

Winter sleeps

Brown bears, American black bears, Asiatic black bears, and polar bears live in parts of the world that have cold winters. These bears sleep through most of winter. They sleep in warm **dens**, or homes. Most bears make dens in caves, in hollow logs, or in deep holes under large tree roots. Polar bears make dens by digging tunnels deep in snow. Bears that sleep through winter eat a lot of food in summer and autumn. They eat to gain fat. They live off the fat while they sleep. When the weather becomes warm in spring, the bears leave their dens and begin searching for food.

Home alone

Adult bears are **solitary animals**. Solitary animals live alone. Each bear lives in its own **home range**. A home range is the area in which an animal lives, finds food, and has babies.

Large or small

Some bears, such as many brown bears, live in habitats with plenty of food. These bears live mainly in small home ranges because they can find food easily. Other bears, such as polar bears, live in home ranges where food is difficult to find. The home ranges of these bears are mainly large because it is easier for them to find food in larger areas.

Many Asiatic black bears live in areas where there is plenty of food. The home ranges of these bears are smaller than the home ranges of the bears that must search for food.

Bear bodies

The bodies of all bears look similar. The main difference between the species of bears is the color of their fur. In some bear species, all the bears have the same fur color. For example, all polar bears have white fur and all giant pandas have black-and-white fur. In other bear species, not all the bears have the same color of fur. For example, American black bears can have brown, black, reddish-brown, tan, gray, or even white fur!

This mother American black bear has white fur. Her babies have black fur.

A bear has sharp teeth for tearing food. It has flat teeth for grinding and chewing food.

A bear has thick fur covering its body.

A bear's claws are long, curved, and sharp.

A bear has strong legs and shoulders. It walks on four paws. It can also stand on its back legs. All bears can run quickly.

Particular paws

Bears that live in different habitats have slightly different paws. Bears that live in cold habitats, such as polar bears, have extra-thick fur on the **soles**, or bottoms, of their paws. This fur keeps a bear's feet warm. Polar bears also have bumps on the soles of their paws. The bumps help the paws grip slippery ice as the bears walk. Bears that climb trees often, such as spectacled bears, have no fur between their toes. Without fur between their toes, the bears can grip the trees with their toes as they climb.

13

The life cycle of a bear

All animals go through a set of changes called a **life cycle**. A bear's life cycle begins when it is born. The bear grows and changes until it is **mature**, or an adult. Mature bears can **mate**, or join together with other bears of the same species to make babies. A new life cycle begins each time a **cub**, or baby bear, is born.

Safe in the den

Baby bears are born in **litters**, or groups. There are often two to three cubs in a litter. A mother bear finds a den before her cubs are born. The cubs are born in the den. Most cubs stay inside the den for several months.

These spectacled bears are safe in their den.

Wake up, Mom!

In cold climates, a mother bear wakes up from her winter sleep as her cubs are born. The mother bear then goes back to sleep. When the cubs want to nurse, they nudge their mother to wake her. The cubs play together in the den. By spring, the weather is warm enough for the mother bear and her cubs to leave the den to search for food.

An American black bear's life cycle

An American black bear cub has no fur on its body when it is born.

A female American black bear is mature when she is three to five years old. A male is mature when he is three to four years old.

When the cub leaves the den with its mother, it begins to eat solid foods. The cub likes to play.

The cub nurses often. It leaves the den for the first time when it is five to seven months old.

15

Bear behavior

Bears use **body language** to **communicate**. Body language is a way of moving. When a bear feels threatened, it stands on its back legs to make itself look bigger. By looking bigger, the bear may scare away other animals.

Stay away!

Bears often use scents to communicate with one another. Bears have an excellent sense of smell. A bear uses scents to keep other bears out of its home range. For example, the bear may rub its body on trees. This rubbing leaves the bear's scent on the trees. The scent is a message to other bears that says, "Stay out of my home!"

This American black bear is standing on its back legs to make itself look larger.

Special sounds

Bears also communicate by making sounds. A mother bear and her babies communicate by making whining and snorting sounds. Bears make some sounds to warn other bears to stay away. If a bear is angry, for example, it clicks its teeth, growls, and roars.

A cub makes whining sounds when it cannot find its mother. The mother bear answers by making snorting sounds. The cub follows the snorting sounds until it finds its mother.

Bear food

Most bears are **omnivores**. Omnivores are animals that eat both plants and animals. Bears eat plant foods such as grasses, berries, and nuts. Many bears also eat small animals such as rabbits, mice, and insects. American black bears and brown bears often catch and eat larger animals, such as young deer or elk.

Sun bears eat termites. These bears have long tongues. They stick their long tongues into termite nests and lick up many insects at once.

Yummy bamboo

Giant pandas eat mainly **bamboo**. Bamboo is a leafy plant. To eat, a panda holds a bamboo stem in its paws. It uses its teeth to pull off the bamboo's leaves before it eats them. Then it puts the stem into its mouth. The panda chews the stem with its large back teeth. Bamboo has few **nutrients**, so giant pandas must eat a lot of bamboo to stay healthy. They can spend up to sixteen hours a day eating!

Frozen food

Polar bears are **carnivores**, or animals that eat other animals. Polar bears sometimes eat walruses and certain types of whales, but they eat mainly seals. A polar bear often hunts seals by waiting next to their **breathing holes**. When a seal sticks its head through a hole to breathe, the polar bear catches and kills it.

Feasting on salmon

Many brown bears live along the western coast of North America. These bears eat salmon. In autumn, thousands of salmon swim from the Pacific Ocean into streams and rivers along the coast. The fish swim to rivers and streams to **spawn**, or lay eggs. This journey is called the **salmon run**. Brown bears catch many salmon during the salmon run.

Shrinking habitats

One of the greatest threats to bears is **habitat loss**. Habitat loss is the destruction of the natural areas where animals live and find food. People **clear**, or remove the plants from, large sections of forests to make room for new roads and buildings.

When people cut down forests, bears and other animals lose their habitats. Along with the habitats, the plants and animals that bears eat are destroyed. Many bears die from **starvation**, or lack of food, when they lose their habitats.

*People have cleared much of this forest to plant **oil palms**. The forest is a sun bear habitat. The sun bears now have fewer places to live and find food. Many hungry sun bears are eating the oil palms. Farmers are killing the bears to stop them from eating these trees.*

Looking for food

When bears cannot find food in their habitats, they often look for food on farms and in cities. Farmers and people in cities often kill hungry bears because they believe the bears will harm people or **livestock**.

These European brown bears are searching for food in a city garbage dumpster.

Hunting bears

Every year, people hunt thousands of bears for sport. Hunters shoot bears or catch them in traps. The traps have sharp spikes. The spikes cause the trapped bears a lot of pain.

Created with cruelty

Bear fur is made into rugs, wall hangings, and clothing. For special events, soldiers in the British Army, shown below, wear hats made from the fur of American black bears. The bears are shot in the spring, when their fur is thickest. In spring, however, most female bears have cubs. When the mother bears are shot for their fur, the cubs are left without their mothers' care. Eventually, the cubs die as well.

Illegal killing

In some countries, it is **illegal**, or against the law, to kill bears. Many people continue to hunt bears, however. People who hunt and kill animals illegally are called **poachers**. Poachers kill bears to sell parts of the bears' bodies, such as the fur.

Giant pandas are protected animals in China. Some poachers, however, still kill giant pandas. The poachers sell the pandas' fur.

Poached for parts

All over the world, poachers kill bears for their paws and for their **organs** called **gallbladders**. Poachers sell bear gallbladders and paws to Asian countries. Some people in these countries believe that bear gallbladders can heal sick people. Scientists have never found this belief to be true, however. People use bear paws to make bear-paw soup. This soup is considered a **delicacy** in many parts of Asia.

Every year in the United States, poachers kill about 3,000 American black bears for their body parts.

Captured bears

In countries such as India, some people **capture** young sloth bears and Asiatic black bears. To capture an animal means to take it out of the wild and keep it in a cage. People force the bears to dance to entertain **tourists**. Tourists pay money to see the bears dance.

A painful life

People treat captured bears very badly. The bears must remain on their back legs while they dance, which is painful for them. Their mouths are tied shut with rope. When they are not performing, the bears are kept in small, damp cages. Many captured bears become sick, but their illnesses are not treated.

This man has a captured sloth bear.
He is forcing the bear to dance.

Bears and bile

In many parts of Asia and South America, people believe that **bile** from a bear's body can be used as medicine. Bile is a liquid created in a bear's gallbladder. Poachers capture bears so that bile can be taken from their bodies.

Removing the bile

The captured bears are locked in small cages. Every day, a tube is shoved into each bear's gallbladder through the bear's belly. The tube sucks out the bile. This cruel practice is very painful to bears. The bile is then sold as medicine.

Many Asiatic black bears, sun bears, sloth bears, and spectacled bears are captured for their bile. This caged bear is an Asiatic black bear cub.

Melting ice

Polar bears are threatened by **global warming**. Global warming is the gradual warming of Earth and its oceans. People cause global warming by burning fuels, such as coal and oil, to heat their homes and run their cars. As the Earth's temperature becomes warmer, **pack ice** melts in the Arctic. Pack ice is huge sheets of ice that float on the Arctic Ocean.

Not enough time

Each year, pack ice freezes in autumn and melts in summer. When the ice is frozen, polar bears travel many miles across it to find and catch seals and other **prey**. The bears need to eat many animals to build up fat for winter. As the Earth becomes warmer, however, the ice is frozen for less time each year. Polar bears have less time to hunt and eat animals. Without enough stored fat, polar bears may starve to death during the winter.

This polar bear has just eaten a seal. The pack ice is melting around the bear, however. The bear may not be able to find more food to eat. Without enough food, it cannot gain the fat it needs to survive the long winter.

Safe places

Many people around the world are working hard to make sure that bears do not become extinct. To protect bears, some countries have created **preserves**. Preserves are areas of land that are protected by governments. On preserves, bears and other animals are safe from poachers and habitat loss. Most countries create preserves in natural areas where the animals already live.

Yellowstone National Park is a preserve in the United States. American black bears and brown bears, shown above, are protected there.

Zoo bears

Some bears live in zoos. Many zoos take good care of animals. They create living areas for the animals that are similar to those of their natural habitats.

Studying bears

Scientists study bears in preserves, in zoos, and in the wild to learn more about them. As they study bears, scientists learn what bears need in order to survive. They also find new ways that people can help protect bears.

These scientists are weighing a sun bear. They have put the bear to sleep so that they can study it.

29

You can help, too!

You can help protect bears, too! Start by learning as much as you can about them. Read books, visit websites, and watch programs about bears. Then share what you have learned with others.

Simple actions that work

You can also help bears by reducing global warming. Simple actions like riding your bike instead of taking a car can make a big difference. Also, make sure you turn off lights in your home when they are not in use. Most important of all, never use or buy products that are made from parts of bears.

By doing simple things to stop global warming, people can help endangered species, such as this sun bear, survive.

Spread the word

There are many ways you can help people learn about endangered bears. Share what you know by writing postcards to your friends with fun facts about bears. Draw pictures of different bear species on the front of the postcards. Another way to spread the word is by making posters about how to protect bears. Display your posters in the hallways of your school. Your local library, zoo, and the Internet are good places to learn more about protecting bears.

Visit these websites to find out about certain bear species:

- www.nationalgeographic.com /kids/creature_feature/0004/ polar.html

- www.panda.org/news_facts/ education/middle_school/ species/omnivores/ bear_brown/index.cfm

- www.bear.org/Kids/ Sounds.html

Glossary

Note: Boldfaced words that are defined in the text may not appear in the glossary.

breathing hole A hole in ice through which a seal sticks its head in order to breathe air

climate The normal weather conditions in an area, including temperature, rainfall, and wind

coast An edge of land that meets an ocean

communicate To send messages to other animals

delicacy A rare, expensive food

Indochina A part of southeast Asia that includes the countries of Cambodia, Laos, Myanmar, Thailand, Vietnam, and part of Malaysia

grasslands Mainly flat areas of land, where many types of grasses grow

livestock Animals, such as cows, which people raise for food

nutrients Substances that living things need to grow and to stay healthy

oil palm A type of tall palm tree

organ A body part, such as the heart, which does an important job

prey Animals that are hunted and eaten by other animals

rain forest A forest that receives at least 100 inches (254 cm) of rain each year

tundra A flat, very cold area in the most northern parts of Canada, Greenland, Russia, and Alaska

tourist A person who travels for fun

warm-blooded Describes animals whose body temperatures stay about the same, no matter how hot or cold their surroundings are

wild Natural areas that are not controlled by people

Index

Printed in the U.S.A.